101

W9-DGE-416

The Story of Science

The Tales Fossils Tell

by Jonathan R. Gallant

BENCHMARK BOOKS

MARSHALL CAVENDISH
NEW YORK

Series Editor: Roy A. Gallant

Series Consultants:

LIFE SCIENCES
Dr. Edward J. Kormondy
Chancellor and Professor of Biology (retired)
University of Hawaii—Hilo/West Oahu

PHYSICAL SCIENCES
Dr. Jerry LaSala
Department of Physics
University of Southern Maine

Benchmark Books
Marshall Cavendish Corporation
99 White Plains Road
Tarrytown, NY 10591-9001

Library of Congress Cataloging-in-Publication Data
Gallant, Jonathan R.
    The tales fossils tell / by Jonathan R. Gallant.
p. cm. — (The story of science)
Includes bibliographical references and index.
Summary: Describes fossils, how they are formed, and what they can tell us about life in the past.
ISBN 0-7614-1153-4
    1. Fossils—Juvenile literature. 2. Paleontology—Juvenile literature. [1. Fossils. 2. Paleontology. 3. Prehistoric animals.] I. Title. II. Series.
QE714.5.G355   2001   56000—dc21   00-020077

Photo research by Linda Sykes Picture Research, Hilton Head, SC
Diagrams on pp. 3, 27, 53, 64–65, 69, by Jeannine L. Dickey
Cover photo: Jeannine L. Dickey
Title page photo of a trilobite fossil by Rich Kroll www.ckart.com/rich
Photo credits: 6 Hanman's Fossils and Minerals (www.hanmansfossils.com); 13 Bibliotheque Nationale, Paris/Archiveo Iconografico, S. A./Corbis; 14, 17, 18 The Granger Collection, New York; 20 Gesner, Conrad, On Fossil Objects, 1551; 22 Colonna, Fabio, 1616; 23 (left) Gesner, Conrad, On Fossil Objects, 1558; 23 (right) Steno, Nicolaus, Dissection of a Shark, 1667; 29 (left) J. C. Carton/CARTO/Bruce Coleman, Inc.; 29 (right) Oxford University Natural History Museum; 30, 31 The Granger Collection, New York; 32 Hanman's Fossils and Minerals (www.hanmansfossils.com); 34 Scheuchzer, Johann, Herbarium of the Deluge, 1709; 37 The Granger Collection, New York; 39 Natural History Museum, Maestricht, The Netherlands; 41 Hanman's Fossils and Minerals (www.hanmansfossils.com); 43 National Maritime Museum/The Art Archive, London; 44 Jeffrey Morgan/Mary Evans Picture Library; 46 Mary Evans Picture Library; 49 Corbis; 51 (left) Peabody Museum of Natural History, Yale University; 51 (right) Mary Evans Picture Library; 54 E. R. Degginger/Bruce Coleman, Inc.; 55 The Granger Collection, New York; 57 John Reader/Photo Researchers; 59, 60 Natural History Museum, London; 63 (large) Photograph by Rich Kroll (www.ckart.com/rich); 63 (inset) 72 Hanman's Fossils and Minerals (www.hanmansfossils.com)

Printed in Hong Kong
6 5 4 3 2 1

For Rosemary, my wife, best friend, and
travel agent extraordinaire

Contents

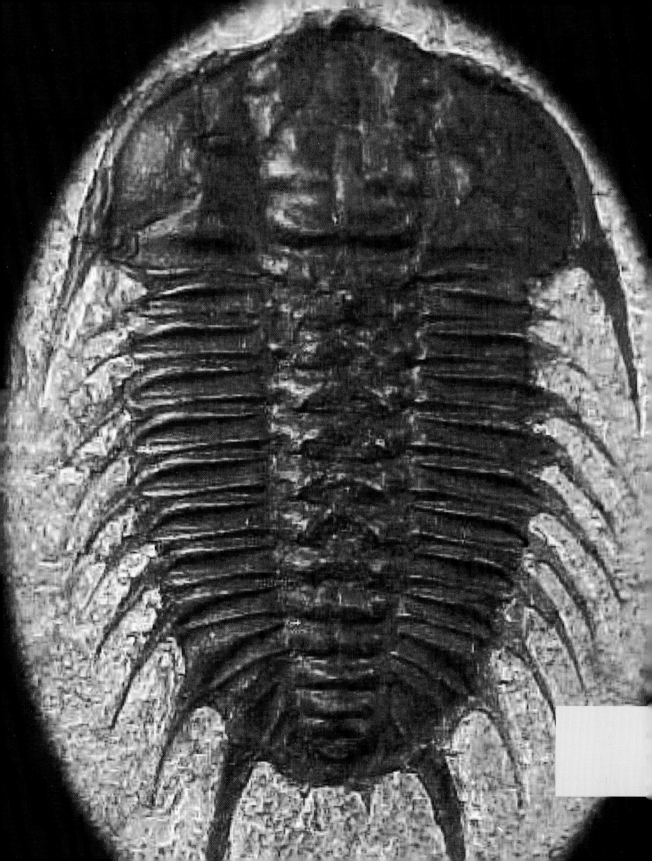

One

Fish Seeds and Living Stones

Imagine that you are on a three-day raft trip down West Virginia's Cheat River. The Cheat runs through the Appalachian Mountains, an area that is poor in money but rich in white water, scenery, and fossils. Over millions of years, the swift-running river water has cut through the land to form a channel. In places, it is over 100 feet (30 meters) below the bridges that span it. As sand, clay, and other sediments long ago accumulated beneath where the river today flows, they pressed down heavily on the sediments beneath. The pressure squeezed out the water and eventually turned the soft sediments into sedimentary rock. Later still, a river cut a deep trench into those ancient rock layers. It is in places like this—sprawling areas with lots of sedimentary rock—that people who study paleontology can find fossils today.

Trilobites appeared in the fossil record in Cambrian times some 530 million years ago. There were more than a thousand different kinds of these hard-shelled creatures that lived in shallow seas. They ranged from microscopic size to about 2 feet (0.6 meters) across. Trilobites were distantly related to later-appearing crabs and scorpions, for example.

Paleontology is the study of ancient life through fossils.

In fact, during one of your rest stops down the Cheat, that is exactly what you decide to do: look for fossils. It just so happens that you brought along your uncle's geologist's hammer, the kind with a point at one end of the head. You chip at the rocks and, lo and behold, you find a piece of a dinosaur bone! Close by, you open another slab of rock and find the imprint of a shell.

Three Questions

What do you know about fossil shells and dinosaur bones? You probably think of dinosaurs as large reptiles that lived millions of years ago. You know that both dinosaur bones and seashells are hard, and that sometimes they lie in the ground for a very long time until they become fossils.

How do you know this? You have probably seen at least one movie that has different kinds of dinosaurs in it, and you have probably visited a museum that has bones and fossil shells on display. So when you found your two fossils, you may have been surprised, but you had a general idea of what they were and how they got there.

Now try to imagine what someone who lived 2,500 years ago would have thought of a dinosaur bone or a shell imprint in rock. Nobody living then had ever studied dinosaurs or fossils the way we do today. No one had even estimated the age of planet Earth. The easiest way to explain stony objects that look like parts of living things would be to find accounts of them in stories and legends. That's just what people did until only about four hundred years ago.

It has been only in the past two hundred years that scientists have come to agree on the answers to three basic questions about fossils:

1. Why do they look like parts of living things?
2. What are they actually made of?
3. How did they get to be where we find them?

Before the year 1800 there were many different answers to those puzzling questions. That was because the people who had answers had different ideas about how the world worked. We call those the questions of *form*, *makeup*, and *position*.

Today, the reason we have learned to draw conclusions about fossils is that people before us struggled long and hard to answer those questions. Then others built on their ideas. Some ideas fit in with what people could observe in nature, but many did not. The characters in our story of fossils include philosophers and scientists who were smart enough to ask the right questions and brave enough to challenge old and common beliefs.

Stories, Legends, and Myths

From the North American West, ancient Sioux legend tells us that what we know today to be dinosaur fossils are the remains of huge serpents that had dug deep into the ground. The Great Spirit did not like strange animals burrowing around, so he killed them with a spear. When American fossil hunters arrived on the scene in the 1800s and started to dig up dinosaur bones by the ton, the Sioux would not help them. They believed doing so would offend the Great Spirit and bring bad luck to the tribe.

The Chinese believed that long ago a natural disaster turned the world upside down and every which way. When this happened, the land and the sea and all living things got mixed together. Over time, water flowed back to the seas and the animals returned to the habitats where they belonged. Fossil animals and plants, says the legend, are the remains of this catastrophe.

The Ancient Greeks and "Fish Seeds"

About 800 B.C., Greek culture began to flourish. While other great civilizations came before ancient Greece, none could match the Greeks' progress in science and mathematics. One reason for this was that the Greeks built on ideas developed by earlier civilizations. For example, Greek mathematics was based on symbols and ideas developed more than a thousand years earlier by the Sumerians and the Babylonians. Another reason was that they kept science separate from the old religious myths and superstitions.

Around 450 B.C., the Greek historian Herodotus was puzzled by fossils he came across. He said that small, round fossils found in Egypt were chunks of food not eaten by the slaves who had built the pyramids long before. On another occasion, after returning from a trip to Arabia, he reported seeing heaps of "backbones and ribs of serpents in such numbers as it is impossible to describe." The bones were not those of recently dead serpents but fossils of extinct animals. However, Herodotus could not have known that since neither the idea nor word for fossil was known to him.

Among the greatest of the Greek philosopher-scientists was Aristotle, who lived from 384 to 322 B.C. He developed theories based on what he could observe in the real world, but he often expressed opinions about matters that could not be tested or proven. For example, he taught that the world had always existed. That notion, called *eternalism*, was to trouble Christian scholars centuries later because it denied that God created the world, as described in the biblical book of Genesis.

Some of the ancient Greeks' ideas about fossils seem strange to us. A fish fossil found in the mountains was said to come from a "fish seed" that made its way from the sea through underground springs and up onto the land. Aristotle agreed with this idea, believing that such marine animal "seeds" were first deposited in wet sand, then grew into adult animals, and later died as stone fish when the sand dried and hardened. Bright gemstones were thought to be earthly reflections of stars. The Greeks regarded the slow-growing stalactites in limestone caves as evidence that Earth is a living being capable of growing things inside itself. Today we know that stalactites are formed by minerals in the water that drips down from limestone cave ceilings.

Two thousand five hundred years ago, philosophers believed that all things on Earth—animals, plants, mountains, rocks, and minerals—had their own ways of living, growing, and dying. Some of those ideas lasted all the way into the 1700s and 1800s. For instance, miners believed that if a worked-out gold or silver mine were left alone long enough, the gold and silver would grow back and so enrich the mine again. The Greeks also regarded crystals as living things that grew. To this day we speak of "growing" crystals in a crystal "garden," but we no longer think of crystals themselves as living forms. Our modern ideas about the differences between living and nonliving things would have sounded as strange to the ancient Greeks as their ideas sound to us today.

The Greek scholar named Xenophanes, who was born around 560 B.C., raised questions that people usually never thought about. He studied fossils that he found in rocks high in the Greek mountains many miles from the sea. He was not at all satisfied with notions such as fish seeds to explain the question of position, or how the fossils got to where they were found. After much thought, he decided that long ago the whole world must have been under a great ocean. Sometime later the land beneath certain parts of the ocean must have been pushed up to become mountains. In the process, many marine creatures were trapped and lifted up with the land. Even though Xenophanes has been praised as the father of geology and paleontology, it took two thousand years for his ideas to be accepted.

The Middle Ages

Our story about fossils next moves ahead to that period in history known as the Middle Ages, which lasted from about A.D. 500 to 1500. It was a period that did not favor scientific investigation or independent thought. In Europe the Christian religion provided answers to any and all questions about the world and man's place in it. The Bible was the main voice of authority and truth. Whenever a scientific discovery or idea conflicted with the Bible, the Bible won out. As a result, scientific inquiry suffered a long period of stagnation. Old books, no matter how learned, that did not praise the glory of God were burned.

All during these desert years of intellectual thought, it was Arab scholars, not Europeans, who preserved and studied the works of the old Greek philosophers and made progress in astronomy and medicine. It also was an Arab mathematician who imported from India into the Western world the concept of zero in mathematics. This provided a new and simple system of writing numbers and manipulating them. Some claim that it was the new mathematics that made possible construction of the many enormous and beautiful medieval cathedrals that stand to this day as reflections of God's glory, and also as monuments to science's dark millennium.

Inside those cathedrals, medieval priests discussed several theories about fossils. One was that they were the remains of creatures the devil had created when he tried to imitate the work of God. Another held that the creatures were left over from God's early attempts to create man and other animals. But that notion was not popular because if God is perfect then He could not have

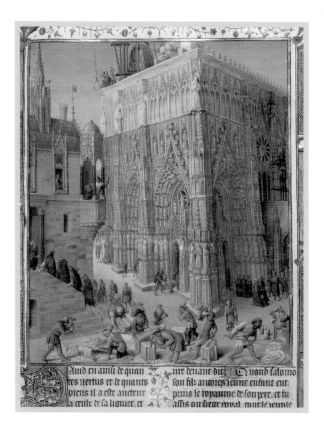

Around the 1400s great cathedrals were being constructed in many large cities in different parts of Europe. During this time in European history, called the Middle Ages, the religious pursuit for the knowledge and glorification of God were considered far more important than the pursuit of learning in science.

blundered in such a way. A third said that fossils were the remains of the animals that were drowned when they did not make it onto Noah's ark during the great flood mentioned in the Bible.

Before the end of the Middle Ages, an Arab physician made an important mistake that greatly influenced later studies of fossils. His name was Abu 'Ali al-Husayn ibn 'Abd Allah ibn Sina, but we know him by his Latin name, Avicenna. He lived from 980 to 1037, and to this day Arab texts call him the "Prince of Learning." At the time, alchemists were talking about ways of changing base metals such as zinc, lead, and copper into the two noble metals gold and silver. Avicenna correctly said that such notions were nonsense, and he would have no part in the discussions. But he carried his thinking a bit too far by incorrectly saying that bone could not be turned into stone, even when he was shown bone-shaped stones and stone fishes and stone clams.

Avicenna reasoned that bronze, for instance, could be given many different shapes, all the while remaining bronze. Perhaps the same was true of stone, he further reasoned. All that was needed was some kind of "shaping force" capable of reshaping a rounded cobblestone, for instance, into a flat piece of stone fish. He further claimed that fossils had never been living animals. Just as Aristotle's teachings were to influence scholars for two thousand years, Avicenna's ideas about fossils were to strongly influence scholars for the next seven hundred years.

Near the end of the Middle Ages, another unusual man enters our story. He was the famous painter, experimenter, inventor, and engineer Leonardo da Vinci, who lived from 1452 to 1519. His scientific curiosity was aroused when he, too, discovered beautifully preserved marine fossils in rocks high up in the mountains of northern Italy. He came across them while digging

The great Italian artist and inventor Leonardo da Vinci, who lived from 1452 to 1519, was among the first to suspect that fossils found high in the mountains were actually the remains of marine animals that had lived long ago in ancient seas. Most people at the time refused to regard fossils as the remains of long-dead animals and plants.

canals and noticed that certain layers of soil and rock became exposed where the river had cut down through the rock. He became convinced that marine fossils contained in the different rock layers were the remains of creatures that had once lived in the ancient seas.

Just as Xenophanes had thought two thousand years earlier, Leonardo believed that long ago the mountains must have been covered by oceans. He reasoned that those ancient oceans must have contained marine animals very similar to the ones living in his time. The resemblance between the fossils and living marine animals was so close that they had to be related in some way. Furthermore, what had once been soft mud that contained the remains of the dead sea creatures had somehow become hard rock. After that, something must have pushed the ocean floor up high out of the water, he said.

Leonardo did not accept the ancient Greek idea of fish seeds, nor did he accept the biblical story of the flood as a way to explain how the fossils got where he found them. After all, he argued, if there were such a world flood that covered the peaks of even the highest mountains, where could all of that water have gone? He did not believe that such a massive flood could possibly have come and gone in only 150 days. He thought his explanation was better because it was based on what he could observe. Many of Leonardo's ideas about how rocks and their fossils were formed foreshadowed theories that would not become popular until more than three hundred years after his death.

Except for a few independent thinkers from the time of the ancient Greeks to the close of the Middle Ages, people's ideas about fossils were based on stories, legends, myths, and superstitions that had been handed down through the ages. The science of paleontology as we know it was still a long way off.

Two

Fossils Pose Questions

How to Start a Revolution

In the early 1500s the scientific study of fossils was given a boost from what might seem an unlikely source—a new invention that had nothing to do with fossils. It was a printing press that allowed letters of the alphabet to be cast as little metal blocks and arranged to spell out words. This movable-type press was made by the German Johannes Gutenberg around 1436. Earlier versions of his invention had already been developed in Korea and China, but Gutenberg's press was better. The first European book ever to be printed with movable type probably was the Mazarin Bible, completed in 1455.

Perhaps more than any other single thing, the Gutenberg press helped bring the Middle Ages to a close by revolutionizing the way new ideas and other information could quickly be made available to people who could read. Gutenberg's printing press unleashed a new way of viewing nature—though the eyes of many different scholars rather than through only the authoritarian eye of

Johannes Gutenberg, who lived from about 1395 to 1468, invented movable type for printing. This meant that many copies of a book could be quickly printed instead of having to be laboriously copied by hand. Gutenberg's presses also helped bring the Middle Ages to a close by spreading new ideas rapidly and widely among scholars.

the church. It was a way that helped change the role of the church from final authority on all matters to simply one voice among many in debates about the nature of the world. Although only one among many, the voice of the church nevertheless remained the strongest one.

How Science Views the World

The English philosopher Francis Bacon, who lived from 1561 to 1626, argued that everything we see in nature must obey natural laws. For example, there must be some way to explain why a rock falls back to Earth after being thrown into the air. There also must be cause for the Moon circling close to Earth instead of flying off into space. But it would be about seventy years before the English physicist Sir Isaac Newton would describe that "natural law" as the force as gravity. Bacon went further, arguing that any natural law we describe must be based on what we are able to observe around us.

Bacon's idea forms the basis of what today is called scientific method, which works something like this: Twenty-five hundred years ago uneducated people believed that Earth was flat because that is what their senses told them. They could neither see nor feel that the world was round. There were mountains and valleys, but these were simply wrinkles on a flat world.

Then along came Aristotle. He observed that during an eclipse of the Moon the shadow Earth cast on the Moon was curved. That curve suggested to him that Earth must be round. If it were flat, its shadow would be a straight line.

The early idea that Earth was round is what scientists call

The English philosopher Francis Bacon, who lived from 1561 to 1626, taught that everything we see in nature must obey natural laws— the roar of a lion, the color of a flower, light from the Sun. Bacon's thinking formed the basis of what today is called scientific method, a way of learning about the world by observing it.

a *hypothesis*. Aristotle next looked for more evidence to support his hypothesis. He found it when he observed how the tall masts of ships disappeared as they sailed out to sea. Rather than vanish from view suddenly, they gradually appeared to become shorter and shorter, as if they were disappearing over the edge of a huge ball. This observation made Aristotle's hypothesis still more believable.

As more and more evidence is found to support a hypothesis, the hypothesis becomes a *theory*. And if a theory stands the test of time, it becomes a *scientific law*, such as the universal law of gravitation or the laws that describe how gases behave when they are heated or compressed.

New Ideas About Fossils

By the mid1500s, printing presses were turning out not only Bibles but also books on scientific subjects, including fossils. One scientist-author was the great Swiss naturalist Conrad Gesner, who lived from 1516 to 1565. In his lifetime, he summarized all of the well-known philosophical texts from Greek, Latin, and Hebrew. His other works included a five-volume encyclopedia of the animal world and a short work titled *On Fossil Objects*. What made his book on fossils remarkable was that it included illustrations. By showing what the objects he was describing looked like, Gesner gave any scientist who opened his book a detailed view of his fossils. Gesner realized that "a picture is worth ten thousand words." This was the first time anyone had treated fossils in this way.

Another new idea was to put fossils on display in museums so that other scientists could study them. The physician Johann Kentmann, who lived from 1518 to 1574, was one of the first to do this. In fact, many of the fossils illustrated in Gesner's book were borrowed from Kentmann's collection. Collectors also began

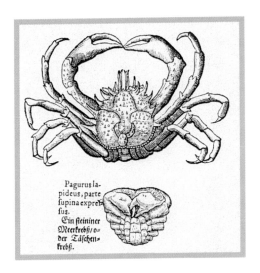

Pagurus la-
pideus, parte
fupina expre-
fus.
Ein fteininer
Meerkrebs / o=
der Täfchen=
krebß.

The Swiss naturalist Conrad Gesner lived from 1516 to 1565. He was among the first to publish a book about fossils with illustrations. In one illustration he compared a fossil crab (bottom) with a living crab that resembled the fossil. This helped convince some naturalists that fossils actually were the remains of animals that had lived very long ago. Many naturalists of the time denied that fossils had ever been living organisms.

to print catalogs that described their fossils and to send the catalogs to scientists in other countries.

An even better way to spread the scientific word was started in 1560 by Giambattista della Porta. His Academy of the Mysteries of Nature gave scientists working far away from one another a way to exchange ideas and discoveries through his Academy's newsletter. Other such academies followed, and soon hundreds of ideas were being rapidly exchanged across Europe. Scientists taking advantage of these academy newsletters were able to learn from each other much more than they possibly could learn by working alone.

Just What *Is* a "Fossil"?

At the time Gesner lived, just about anything that came out of the ground was called a fossil. In those days, the meaning of the word *fossil* was the same as its Latin ancestor fossilis, meaning anything that is dug up.

Fossils ranged along a broad scale of those dug-up things. At one end were stony remains that looked like animals of some sort but that bore little or no resemblance to the animals then living. At the other end were stony remains that looked very much like certain animals then living. Then along the middle there were sort of "in-between" critters.

Because the term fossil included so many things, scientists for a long time did not single out what today we call true fossils. A hangover of this verbal confusion is with us today when we use the expression "fossil fuels," meaning coal and petroleum. Neither coal nor petroleum is a fossil. This is an example of how the meaning of a word can determine how we see the world around us. It would take a creative thinker to loosen, if not break, this language logjam faced by scientists of the 1600s.

One such thinker was Fabio Colonna, who lived from 1567 to 1650. Like other naturalists of his time, Colonna had a wide range of interests, especially biology and fossils. In 1616 he published a book that grouped fossils right along with living organisms that the fossils resembled. Although many other scientists of the time believed that some fossils probably came from once-living plants and animals, none had made the connection so clearly or convincingly. Colonna's new approach changed the way many naturalists regarded fossils. Even so, some still thought of fossils as growing from seeds mysteriously planted in rock, especially those fossils that looked very different from living plants and animals. Colonna's convincing biological evidence that at least some fossils came from once-living creatures found more favor among biologists than among geologists. The debate over fossils having an *organic* (living) rather than an *inorganic* (nonliving) origin was to go on for many more years.

One person who at least chipped away at the old belief of stonelike animals growing inside of stones was Niels Stensen, an independent thinker better known as Steno. He lived from 1638

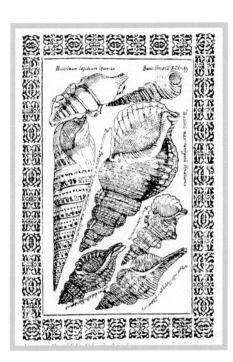

Fabio Colonna lived from 1567 to 1650. In his 1616 book about fossils, he showed a number of living marine organisms and included among them a fossil organism (top left). The similarity between the fossil and living species helped convince naturalists that fossils, indeed, were once living creatures and not just curious rocks.

to 1686. Originally from Denmark, Steno moved to Florence, Italy, to do medical research when he was twenty-seven years old. He became so famous as an anatomist that when a huge shark was hauled ashore by some fishermen in a nearby village, the grand duke of Tuscany ordered that its head be cut off and taken to Steno for study.

Steno immediately noticed that the shark's teeth were remarkably similar to objects called tongue-stones that he had seen in fossil collections. At that time, people thought that tongue-stones were just smooth, pointed rocks that had some-how grown inside other rocks where they were found. Here was an example of those who stubbornly held to the old Greek idea of the inorganic origin of fossils. The more Steno studied tongue-stones, the more evidence he found of decay-just like that found in the dead shark's teeth. He soon became convinced that all tongue-stones came from dead sharks. His idea agreed with Colonna's suspicion that at least some fossils were organic in origin and so came from things that once were alive. They were not simply stones within stones.

Meanwhile, in England, a scientist named Robert Hooke came to the same conclusion. Hooke, who lived from 1635 to 1703, used wood instead of sharks' teeth to support his hypothesis. He was an enthusiastic user of another recent invention, the

Gesner's illustration of 1558 may have been the first to show a fossil shark tooth along with an illustration of the living animal whose teeth very closely resembled the fossil tooth.

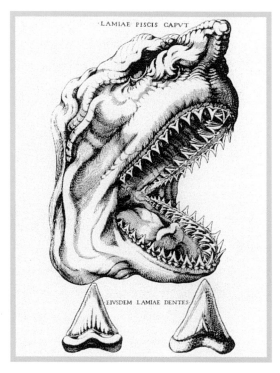

"Tongue-stones" were once thought to be smooth, pointed stones that had grown inside other rocks. A young anatomist named Steno, who lived from 1638 to 1686, showed that the tongue-stones actually were the fossilized teeth of sharks.

23

microscope. He believed that the microscope would unlock secrets of the natural world that he and his colleagues could not even begin to imagine. In his book *Micrographia*, published in 1665, Hooke pointed out that fossilized wood shows signs of decay when examined under the microscope. Like Steno before him, Hooke concluded that the fossils he studied came from actual trees and not mysterious seeds of stone.

Answers to the Three Questions—and Objections

By the mid-1600s, the leading scientists of the time had come to think of fossils a bit differently from the ways fossils had been regarded by scholars of the Middle Ages and by the Greeks still earlier. But just how different were the views of Colonna, Steno, and Hooke on the questions of form, makeup, and position from earlier views?

Form Scientists of the 1600s had come to recognize that some fossils came from once-living things. This was important because it separated organic fossils from all other "dug up" things just called fossils. Few believed that tongue-stones or a piece of fossil wood had actually grown inside a rock. Colonna, Steno, and Hooke all hypothesized that organic fossils got their forms from liquids and soft, muddy solids that hardened in the ground. But just how they hardened, no one at the time could say.

Although scientists like Colonna, Steno, and Hooke understood that there was a connection between some fossils and things that were once alive, they could make that connection only for the most obvious cases. Many fossils didn't look anything like living creatures. And that was disturbing because the idea of extinction was unknown at the time. So when the fossil of a shell of an extinct marine organism was discovered, some scientists asked: If this is from a dead animal, where is the living animal?" To them, the lack of any living examples was proof that the fossils could not have come from living things. They must somehow have grown inside the rocks.

Makeup When it came to questions of how rocks or fossils are formed, Seventeenth Century European Scientists did not know much more that the philosopher-scientists of ancient Greece knew two thousand years before them. Not much change here. In the 1600s, nobody knew how rocks or shell fossils, for instance, were formed. So when they heard the arguments of Steno and others, some asked, AIf these fossils come from shells, where is the shell? I find only rock." Scientists still had not asked questions about how rocks are formed. Like the idea of extinction, the idea of makeup was a problem for future scientists to solve.

Position How did sharks' teeth and seashells, for example, wind up high in the mountains? The most common explanations of the day were the biblical flood and earthquakes. But neither one seemed able to explain why certain types of fossils were usually found only in layers of certain rock at certain depths in the ground. Hooke supposed that a powerful earthquake long ago had caused fossils to be "thrown up" onto the land. Some objected by saying that the same kinds of fossils should then be found everywhere and all mixed up. They clearly were not. Like the question of makeup, the question of position would have to wait for geologists of the future.

Let's now find out why those scientists of the future were first baffled by, but eventually came to solve, the two major problems of extinction and position. At times tempers flared and words were hurled like bricks.

Three

Fossils Provide Answers

The 1600s were a time for asking questions about what fossils actually were and how they came to be where they were found. The 1700s were a time for answers to those and other questions about fossils and what they implied about Earth's dark and mysterious past.

Steno, Colonna, Hooke, and others in the 1600s had no idea that the fossils they held in their hands and described in their catalogs told the story of Earth and its ancient pageant of life.

Extinctions and Earth's Age

One of the problems that kept troubling naturalists into the 1700s was the strangeness of some fossils. They were willing to admit that fossils that closely resembled living animals might well be the

Fossils enable scientists to build accurate models of animals that lived millions of years ago. Large-eyed cephalopods made the dimly-lit sea floor their home during the Devonian Period some 380 million years ago.

organic remains of those animals. But what about all the fossils that didn't look anything like creatures then living? Where were their living relatives, if indeed there were any? One answer was that they probably still existed somewhere in the world but no one had discovered them yet—in the depths of unexplored oceans or in the forbidding forests of South America or Africa. Although it was an answer, it wasn't a very convincing one. It was more a way to avoid the problem. A better explanation was that the animals had died out, or become extinct, long ago.

Unfortunately, at this point religion got in the way of science. The argument went something like this: Since the time of the biblical Creation, all of the plants and animals created by God must surely still exist. The very idea of extinction suggested that those animal and plant species that had become extinct were in some way imperfect. Otherwise, why would they die out? Since God had created all living things and was now watching over them, then He had somehow blundered and so was imperfect. The idea

of an imperfect God was unacceptable to the church, and so the notion of extinction was also unacceptable. If extinction was not possible, then it was not possible to accept the organic origin of those strange fossils with no apparent living relatives.

There was another roadblock to the idea of extinction: time. In the 1600s, some scholars were puzzling over the age of Earth. Few even imagined the planet's actual great age, although they believed it was "old." Just how old? Among the religious scholars bent on solving the age problem was James Ussher, archbishop of Armagh, Ireland, and John Lightfoot, of England's Cambridge University. In 1650, they claimed that the world began at 9:00 A.M. on October 23 in the year 4004 B.C. That date was based on events described in the Bible and by accepting every word of the Bible as fact. At the time, the Bible was looked on as one of the only trustworthy sources of information about Earth's early history and the early history of life. Oriental sources suggesting that Earth was much older seemed unacceptable, as was Aristotle's notion of eternalism, which said that Earth had always existed.

So if the Bible said that God created the world and all its living creatures at just about the same time only a few thousand years ago, that left no possibility for a world very much older than its living beings. After all, if God created the world for man, what would be the point of having an Earth much older than the humans for which it was created? So went the religious argument for an Earth only about six thousand years old. That seemed hardly old enough for extinctions to have taken place. The study of fossils was soon to change that notion.

Several scientists just before and just after 1700 became fascinated with the problem of Earth's age. At one end of the time scale was Aristotle's notion of eternalism. At the opposite end was the relatively young age implied by the Bible. While many felt that the biblical age of about six thousand years was too young, others felt uncomfortable with the idea of eternalism. In the early 1700s the astronomer Edmond Halley estimated Earth's age by calculating how long it must have taken the seas to accumulate their large amounts of salts. The age he came up with was much greater than six thousand years. However, it seems that Halley wanted to disprove the idea of an eternal Earth more than he

 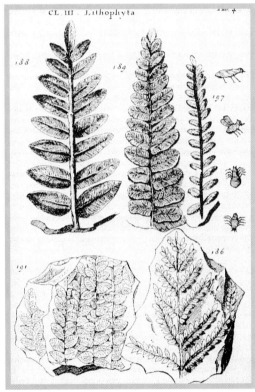

Around 1700 scientists were baffled by plant fossils, which were mere impressions lacking any actual plant material. These drawings were made in 1699 by Edward Lhwyd who couldn't explain them since they did not resemble any plants known at that time. The ferns in the photograph at left come from France's coal fields. They date from the Carboniferous Period some 300 million years ago.

wanted to stretch the age arrived at by biblical scholars. Most scientists of that time would not propose an age for Earth of even millions of years; it strayed too far from the Bible. Besides, there was no hard evidence to support such an idea.

Buffon's *Natural* History

The greatest naturalist of the 1700s was Georges-Louis Leclerc, Comte de Buffon, who lived from 1707 to 1788. Buffon was a great believer in doing experiments to set matters straight. He found it hard to believe that the great Archimedes had actually set fire to a Roman fleet of ships by focusing the Sun's rays from a distance of a "bowshot", as had been claimed. To find out if such a feat could be accomplished, he arranged 168 mirrors in a frame and reflected the Sun's rays onto some wooden planks 150 feet (46 meters) away. The planks burst into flame. In the same way, he next set fire to a pile of wood chips, sulfur, and charcoal 250 feet (76 meters) away.

Buffon's abilities as a fire starter were exceeded by his

Count Georges Louis Leclerc de Buffon, who lived from 1707 to 1788, was among the last of the natural historians who tried to write a sweeping account of Earth's history. The new scientists, represented by Cuvier, felt it was more important to collect, analyze, and compare thousands of fossils and so try to learn about past life forms.

Buffon was a great believer in doing experiments to set matters straight. He found it difficult to believe that the great Archimedes had actually set fire to Roman ships by focusing the Sun's rays on them from a distance of a "bowshot," as had been claimed. To find out if such a feat could be accomplished, he arranged 168 mirrors in a frame and reflected the Sun's rays onto some wooden planks 150 feet (46 meters) away. The planks burst into flame.

abilities as a naturalist. During his later years, he prepared a monumental forty-four-volume description of the animal kingdom and a history of Earth. He concluded that Earth must be at least 75,000 years old, despite what the Bible might say. He further said that geological processes then at work could perfectly well explain the positions of fossils found on the land. Although he didn't actually deny the biblical flood, he said there was no scientific need for it, and therefore, it could be ignored. Toward the end of his life, Buffon became convinced that millions of years of geologic change must have been needed to account for all of the rock strata to have been piled layer on layer through the ages. And just as important (as fossils were later to show) Earth must have had a very ancient history long before humans ever appeared on the scene.

Buffon's important work was, if anything, a bit too grand for the new naturalists who came after him. The story he tried to tell was too sweeping. For one thing, he had divided Earth's history into seven stages. To many, that sounded too much like the biblical account of Creation. For another thing, Buffon had tried to sketch on one canvas the entire history of Earth and its life. It was all too general, and it lacked the thousands of documented observations needed to make the story convincing.

Georges Buffon's towering work over a period of some fifty years did not mark the beginning of a new era in the story of fossils. Instead, it marked the close of an old one. However, one large idea of Buffon's that marched forcefully into the new era was that the study of rocks and the fossils they contained would one day unravel that long period of history before the appearance of humans.

Ants, flies, and other insects have become stuck to pitch oozing out of trees. After the pitch completely enclosed them, it then hardened into stonelike beads called amber. Many thousands of years later these fossilized insects may be found and so add to our knowledge of past life.

Four

New Views, New Naturalists

Around the time Buffon was writing his grand overview of Earth's history, an English clergyman named Thomas Burnet (about 1635–1715) was trying to solve the puzzle of Earth's jumbled surface features—mountains here, seas there, valleys and other features seemingly all mixed up. The year was 1681. He, like so many other English geologists, tried to explain Earth's surface features by following the biblical account of the deluge, or flood.

A Beginning for Earth

Burnet imagined that Earth was once a smooth-skinned planet of rock partly filled with water. After many years of being heated by the Sun, Earth's crust cracked and broke open. Enormous blocks of rock and soil plunged into the subterranean ocean. Water surged out in gigantic waves and pounded its way over Earth's smooth surface. Mountains were raised, and deep valleys were cut into the land. Great chunks of earth were folded, tumbled, and twisted this way and that.

This catastrophe, in Burnet's thinking, was the biblical flood. It changed Earth from a smooth and orderly paradise into a shattered and chaotic globe. Although many scholars and clergymen attacked Burnet's ideas, others liked them, especially the idea of a world flood since a flood was part of biblical history.

It was the French philosopher René Descartes (1596–1650) who in 1644 had first suggested the idea of a planet going through a catastrophic flood stage. He insisted that he was not talking specifically about Earth, rather about an imagined planet,

Until the mid-1700s, the flood, as described in the Bible, seemed to be the only way to explain how marine fossils could be found high and dry in the mountains. In this engraving from a book published in 1709 notice Noah's ark to the right of the mountain peak island. Also notice marine shells being cast onto the land in the foreground.

a planet that at first was a hot globe of rock and later cooled. On cooling, Descartes said, the planet's crust broke open and released the "fluid layer" of the biblical "great deep," that is, the universal flood. So people now lived on a "mere ruin or broken globe." Hooke, Burnet, and others liked Descartes' idea so much that they applied it to Earth, ignoring his warning that he was describing an imaginary planet.

While Burnet was working out his ideas, the Scottish geologist and philosopher James Hutton around the mid-1700s looked to a less catastrophic explanation for the arrangement of rock and soil layers, or *strata*. Hutton, who lived from 1726 to 1797, traveled throughout Great Britain studying rocks in mountains, in seaside cliffs, and buried under fields. What he saw made him believe that all rocks were subject to forces of nature that change them ever so slowly. Wind and water cause erosion, materials on top of sediments change the sediments into stone, and pressure and heat deep inside Earth change one kind of rock into another. These forces act so slowly, Hutton argued in 1785, that it must have taken many millions of years for Earth to have become the way it is today. Hutton's argument pushed Earth's age back still further in time.

He said that the forces that mold and change Earth's surface today have been operating over periods with "no vestige of a past, and no prospect of an end." His idea of *uniformitarianism*, as it came to be called, held that "the present is the key to the past." Some geologists of the time found Hutton's idea of a near eternity of gradual change hard to accept. It smacked of eternalism. Over parts of Europe there were many signs that only a few thousand years earlier there had been sudden and drastic geologic upheavals. Today we know that those upheavals were brought on by the last ice age. The idea of gradual change was soon to be vigorously challenged by a true giant of geology and paleontology.

Meanwhile, however, the German geologist Abraham Gottlob Werner, born in 1750, was trying to understand what forces had formed the rock strata he observed in mine shafts in his native Saxony. Werner was not a traveler. He assumed that the same kinds of strata must exist the world over, and that they were formed one atop another in the same order in China or India, for instance, as in Saxony. It seemed logical to suppose that a vast ocean had flooded the world and then dried up, time and again, flood after flood throughout Earth's history. The idea of gradual, long-term change seemed hard to accept. Each time there was a flood, Werner reasoned, a new layer of rocks and soil and mountains would be formed fairly quickly. He saw Earth composed of onion-like layers, each formed during a given flood period of geologic time.

The idea of rock strata as a key to Earth's geological and biological history took a new turn around 1800 with the work of the English engineer William Smith. His success in building canals depended largely on a knowledge of the different rock layers he dug through. As he studied different strata, he noticed that many had fossils. He also noticed that any single layer usually had pretty much the same groups of fossils. Each younger rock layer higher up, and the older rock layers below, had different kinds of fossils. Soon, Smith became so skillful that whenever he saw a fossil he could tell which layer of rock it came from.

Catastrophism and Rapid Change

At about the same time Smith was studying fossils in England, the French geologist and anatomist Georges Cuvier was studying and mapping the fossil-bearing rock strata that surrounded Paris. Cuvier, who lived from 1769 to 1832, was one of the most gifted scientists in history. It was he who so vigorously challenged Hutton's notion of uniformitarianism and slow change.

Like Smith, Cuvier saw that any particular fossil was found only in certain rock layers and not in others. As he arranged his collections of fossils in the same order as the rock strata from which they came, his anatomist's eye noticed that the fossils changed in an orderly way from one layer to the next. Fossils from the higher, and therefore younger, rock layers were more similar to modern forms of life than fossils from older rock layers lower down.

Cuvier's work convinced him beyond a doubt that animal species throughout time had become extinct. He could not accept the argument that somewhere in the wilds of Africa or the depths of the Pacific, living animals just like those strange-looking fossil creatures one day would be found. Earlier, one geologist had

The French paleontologist Georges Cuvier lived from 1769 to 1832. One of his most important accomplishments was to convince other scientists that after very long periods of time most plants and animals become extinct. The idea of extinction was not at all popular among scientists because it suggested that God's creation of animals or plants was in some way imperfect or incomplete. Such a notion was unacceptable to the church.

explained away those "strange" fossil critters by saying that from time to time "nature is playful" and creates sports.

If animals had become extinct throughout Earth's long history, then how did Cuvier account for new species that replaced the older ones? And how did he explain the gradual change in anatomy from older to more recent species, as so clearly were revealed in the fossil record? Earlier, Hooke had correctly suspected that extinction was a rule commonly followed in nature. He also believed it was possible that new species come into being and replace the older ones, possibly in a way similar to the practice of breeding new varieties of cattle and dogs. Here was a glimmering of the idea of evolution. If Hooke had lived another one hundred fifty years, he would have been very pleased.

Extinction and Evolution

Cuvier could not accept the idea of evolution. It had seriously, but unconvincingly, been proposed in the early 1800s by the highly respected Jean-Baptiste Lamarck. Lamarck imagined a very ancient Earth. He said that all animals and plants ever created slowly changed, or evolved, and that such change required great lengths of time. No animal or plant ever went extinct. It simply gradually changed in form. Thus every creature ever created by God still lived; only its "costume" had changed.

Cuvier dismissed Lamarck's theory of evolution for two reasons. One, Cuvier had shown convincingly that extinctions in nature are the rule. Second, he regarded Lamarck as he had regarded Buffon. Lamarck's overview of evolution was too sweeping, too grand, too lacking in detailed evidence. Where were the hundreds of observations needed to support such a grand theory? Cuvier had built his theories on the basis of studying thousands of fossils. Cuvier did, however, agree with Lamarck that Earth was very ancient, some "thousands of centuries old."

Cuvier firmly believed that animal and plant species were unchangeable, or *immutable*. Once created by God, each species remained forever the same, he said. When asked to explain why an older layer of rock contained plant and animal fossils that never were found in younger layers near the top, Cuvier had a ready answer, of sorts. He said that a flood or some other catastrophe struck and killed all living things in a certain region. Then, after the catastrophe, new animals and plants from other parts of the world migrated to the stricken region and repopulated it with new and different kinds of living things. When other catastrophes occurred,

People could no longer deny that species became extinct, with evidence such as this giant lizardlike jaw uncovered in Maestricht, the Netherlands just before 1800. It was Cuvier's skills in anatomy that correctly placed the jaw bone in history as a great lizard, which he termed a monasaur.

the same process of repopulation followed, and this accounted for each rock layer having its own distinctive kinds of fossils.

Or so it seemed. Cuvier's explanation failed entirely to account for the fact that the fossils from the younger rock layers were more similar to modern forms of life than fossils from deeper layers. Nevertheless, the idea of the wholesale destruction of populations of animals and plants from time to time appealed to many. It became known as the principle of *catastrophism,* although Cuvier himself used the word *revolutions.*

Cuvier explained it in these words: "The dislocation and overturning of older strata show without any doubt that the causes which brought them into the position which they now occupy were sudden and violent. . . . The evidences of those great and terrible events are everywhere to be clearly seen by anyone who knows how to read the record of the rocks."

Cuvier set down many of his ideas in a book with the title *Discourse on the Revolutions of the Surface of the Globe.* The book was highly regarded both by the public and in scientific circles throughout Europe and abroad. The English edition of the book was edited by the Scottish geologist Robert Jameson, who took it on his own to change not only the title, to *Theory of the Earth,* but also some of the contents. For one thing, he added many editorial notes of his own creation. One even went so far as to explain how Cuvier's most recent "revolution" actually was the biblical flood and so provided evidence of the scientific truth of the Bible. Had Cuvier been aware of this he would have been furious, for he firmly believed in keeping religion and science apart. However, since most of the English-speaking world learned about Cuvier's ideas through Jameson's editions, readers assumed just the opposite, that Cuvier had set out to lend scientific support to the Bible. Nothing could have been further from the truth, but it pleased English geologists who, more than many geologists elsewhere, yearned for harmony between science and Scripture.

On the topic of evolution, to his dying day, Cuvier never came around to accepting the idea that animal and plant species do actually evolve. Had he lived another twenty or so years, he might well have changed his mind. It was in 1859 when the English naturalist Charles Darwin published what became one of the greatest scientific books of all time. Titled *On the Origin of Species*, it explained Darwin's theory of evolution. Its detail and the tales it told would have fascinated Cuvier. It solved Cuvier's puzzle of why fossils from younger rock layers were always more similar to modern life forms than were fossils from deeper layers.

Fossil imprints of animal tracks and leaves, for instance, are an important part of the fossil record. The "leaf slab" shown here contains several fossil imprints about 45 million years old. The leaf (genus Platanus) numbered 1 is incomplete, but the one numbered 2 is remarkably well preserved. A long willow leaf is also visible in the slab just above the number 1.

Five

Voyage of HMS *Beagle*

Two days after Christmas in 1831, HMS *Beagle* sailed from England on a southwesterly course. Its destination: South America. One of the *Beagle*'s missions was to study the biology and geology of South America's west coast and some of its nearby islands. Robert Fitzroy, Royal Navy captain and skipper of the *Beagle*, was an intense young man in his twenties and a religious fanatic who believed in the literal truth of the Bible.

One of the passengers was a twenty-one-year-old student who was much interested in geology and natural history. He also planned to become a minister. In his appointment as ship's naturalist, he was ready to fulfill one of Captain Fitzroy's expectations— to prove once and for all the scientific truth of the biblical story of

Darwin's ship HMS Beagle enters the waters off Tierra del Fuego, South America's southernmost point. Darwin spent nearly five years aboard the Beagle collecting, studying, and shipping thousands of plant and animal specimens back to England for further study.

Creation. This young student expected the plants, animals, and fossils he was to collect and study during the five-year voyage to provide the evidence. His name was Charles Darwin (1809–1882). At the time he seemed comfortable enough with his assignment, but as he gathered his specimens and later studied them back in England, he came to disagree with Fitzroy's ideas about Earth's history.

Darwin's Search for the Truth

From reading the works of the English geologist Charles Lyell, Darwin understood that an ability to read the geological record accurately was essential to an understanding of the fossil record.

With a passion for collecting, Darwin littered the *Beagle*'s decks with specimens brought up in his tow nets. At each island stop, and ashore for weeks at a time on the South American

Charles Darwin, the greatest naturalist of all time, lived from 1809 to 1882. For twenty years he worked out his principle of evolution through natural selection, although he was not the first to propose that species evolve. Although some scientists of the time scoffed at Darwin's ideas, virtually every biologist living today recognizes the fact of evolution.

mainland while Fitzroy was off surveying, Darwin collected hundreds of insects, small mammals, reptiles, plants, and fossils—anything that could be preserved for shipment back home to his college for further study. All the while, he recorded his observations in fine detail.

At Punta Alta, overlooking the harbor of Bahia Blanca, Darwin made his first important find when he pried out fossils of an extinct giant rodent (*Toxodon*) resembling a hippopotamus, and another extinct giant (*Megatherium*) related to the sloth. Darwin wondered why these extinct species should so closely resemble species living today.

The more Darwin observed and marveled over the close

relationships between the dead and the living, the clearer it became to him that species changed over time, or evolved. They changed in response to their changing environments. Those species that had adapted to their environments survived. Those that could not adapt became extinct. Darwin was fascinated by the "magic" of adaptation. Everywhere he looked he found life in splendid variety. "We may well affirm," he wrote, "that every part of the world is habitable! Whether lakes of brine, or those underground ones hidden beneath volcanic mountains, or warm mineral springs, or the wide expanse and depths of the ocean, or the upper regions of the atmosphere, and even the surface of perpetual snow—all support living things."

As the *Beagle* made its way up the west coast of South America, Darwin went ashore on the Galápagos Islands to observe and collect. He became especially interested in fourteen species of finches that lived on the various islands. As he collected specimens for shipment home, he kept all the birds from James Island in one bag, those collected on Chatham Island in another bag, and so on. The general features of all the finches— body shape, shortish tails—were similar; they all built the same kind of nest and laid the same number and color eggs; and they resembled the finches of the South American mainland.

When Darwin began to compare the finches in his collecting bags, he was astonished to discover that the finches from Charles Island belonged to one species, those from Albemarle Island to another, those from Chatham to still another, and so on. What distinguished the finch species was the shape of their beaks. Some had short, powerful beaks for crushing tough seeds. Another species had a long, slender beak suited to picking insects out of crevices in the bark of trees. Each species had evolved a special way of feeding that made it better able to

The differences in beak structure of various species of Galapagos finches convinced Darwin that each species was adapted to eat certain kinds of food. Whereas one species had a strong short beak for breaking open nuts, another had a long slender beak suited for picking insects out of crevices in the bark of trees. In this way two such species did not compete with each other for food.

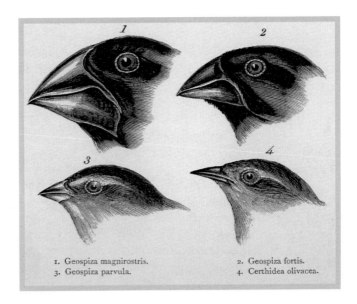

1. Geospiza magnirostris.
3. Geospiza parvula.
2. Geospiza fortis.
4. Certhidea olivacea.

survive on one island than on another. All the island species of finch that Darwin studied had evolved from an original ancestor species from the mainland.

Putting It All Together

The *Beagle* returned to England on October 2, 1836. Using the ideas of scientists and other great thinkers before him, Darwin carefully built his case for the evolution of animals and plants for the next 20 years. One of those earlier thinkers was a British economist named Thomas R. Malthus. Some forty years earlier, Malthus had pointed out that human populations tend to grow faster than the supplies of the food they eat. This suggested to Darwin that competition for food is an unchanging fact of life. It also suggested that the strongest, or smartest, individuals are the ones that survive.

During those years, others also were thinking about evolution, quite apart from Darwin's work. One was an English compiler of encyclopedias named Robert Chambers. In 1844 he published a book with the title *Vestiges of the Natural History of Creation*. Although it was still widely believed that Earth and all its creatures were the handiwork of a divine Creator, Chambers proposed that Earth's living beings all evolved through time due to gradual geological change. Chambers was not a scientist and so failed to strengthen his argument with the kinds of facts and observations that Darwin was sorting out. Even so, *Vestiges* became very popular, although it outraged the British religious community for suggesting that forces other than God could have anything to do with the Creation. Interestingly, the book also anticipated a number of Darwin's ideas.

Alfred Russel Wallace, a biologist living in the East Indies in the late 1850s, was thinking along the same lines as Darwin. In 1858 he sent a short paper that he had written on his theory of evolution to Darwin for comment. Darwin saw many of his own ideas in Wallace's paper, so the two papers were presented together in London. As sometimes happens in the world of science, two people had independently developed the same theory. Evolution by natural selection was an idea whose time had come.

When Darwin's book, *On the Origin of Species by Means of Natural Selection*, was published in late 1859, it became the most important book in biology ever to be published, and it remains so to this day. The first printing of 1,250 copies sold out the first day and turned the whole science of biology upside down.

Darwin had built his case for evolution over many years by making thousands of detailed observations. In the same way, Cuvier had made his case for extinctions. Darwin's theory of evolution quickly won the respect of biologists the world over and today is regarded by nearly all biologists as fact and as the unifying principle underlying all of biology.

Six

Dinosaurs, a Hoax, and Lucy

In the years before Darwin's *Origin of Species* was published, paleontologists were turning up fossil bones of strange animals by the thousands and trying to make sense of them. The ones deeper and deeper in the lower strata resembled living species less and less. Interestingly, human fossils were never found in those ancient layers. If God had created humans right along with other animals, then where were the humans? It seemed that man came along much later in Earth's history than the critters Cuvier was digging out of the ground around Paris.

Cuvier had dug up a mammoth and other mammals. There were also fossils of strange-looking reptiles, fishes, and even a bird. Mammals seemed to be more recent creatures, since they were never found among the deeper fossils of reptiles and fishes. Cuvier was fascinated when he found a giant crocodile, which later was named a mosasaur. His expert eye as an anatomist saw that a birdlike fossil found in Bavaria was actually a flying reptile. He uncovered the bones of an ichthyosaur. A geologist in England assembled the fossil bones of what turned out to be the marine reptile plesiosaur. The English geologist William Buckland had identified the 40-foot-long (12-meter) *Megalosaurus*. The amateur English geologist Gideon Mantell later found some fossil teeth that belonged to a new type of dinosaur, the huge plant-eating reptile *Iguanodon*. Dinosaurs, (meaning "terrible lizards"), were becoming the rage.

Battle of the Bones

The study of dinosaur fossils erupted explosively in the United States in the late 1800s. As sometimes happens in science, two individuals become fierce competitors. In this case, each wanted to find more and bigger dinosaur bones than the other and so go down in history as the champion of dinosaurs.

Their story begins with the American paleontologist Othniel Marsh, who lived from 1831 to 1899, a professor at Yale University, and the English zoologist Thomas Henry Huxley, who was Darwin's major supporter. Marsh had assembled a remarkable collection of horse fossils showing that modern horses had evolved from horselike animals living millions of years earlier.

A museum worker puts the finishing touches on a dinosaur skull while T. rex, *in the background, looks on.*

When Huxley saw Marsh's collection during a tour of North America in 1876, he hypothesized the existence of an even earlier ancestor of the modern horse. Two months later the fossil remains of Huxley's imagined ancestor horse were dug up. Here was still more solid evidence that animals evolved through time.

But Marsh's chief interest was dinosaurs. So was that of his bitter rival Edward Cope. Both were men of wealth, fiercely independent, proud, and scholars with a passion for dinosaurs. During his lifetime (1840–1897), Cope published 1,400 scholarly papers and books, a remarkable achievement. The two spent nearly thirty years trying to outexplore, outdig, and outdiscover each other in the Rocky Mountains. The feud began in the late 1860s and became the most bitter one in the history of science, but it resulted in a boon to the discovery of dinosaur fossils.

In 1877 two schoolteachers informed Marsh and Cope about rich dinosaur finds they had made in Colorado, one near Morrison and the other near Cañon City. Those discoveries touched off the race between the two men to win the dinosaur lottery. Theirs was a private war and was financed out of their own pockets. Cope's bones from near Cañon City were bigger than Marsh's bones from the Morrison site, which infuriated Marsh. But then Marsh gained the upper hand when he was put onto fossils at Como Bluff, Wyoming. Marsh was told that the bones "extended for seven miles and are by the ton . . . and easy to get out." And so the rivalry continued through the years.

The richness of dinosaur bones in Marsh's favorite hunting grounds near Como Bluff cannot be exaggerated. For instance, on June 12, 1898, a team of paleontologists from New York's American Museum of Natural History was out looking near Laramie, Wyoming, for good places to dig for bones. After several days without much luck, they were amazed to stumble onto a hillside littered with fragments of large dinosaur bones. Off to one side was something even more surprising. A local shepherd had collected some of the biggest bones and used them to build a cabin. With that many bones lying about on top of the ground, what might be buried just beneath the surface, they wondered? They struck it rich, finding a mine of dinosaur bones. They ended up with 60,000 pounds (27,220 kilograms) of dinosaur fossils, enough to fill two freight cars. The bones were shipped to the museum, where some of them are on display today as fossils from the Bone Cabin Quarry.

The Puzzle of Humans

By the 1800s the discovery of fossils that appeared to be human-like were raising many questions. What was man's place in the

With hammer in hand and pistols in his belt, Othaniel Marsh poses with a group of his students before departing for the West on a dinosaur fossil hunt. Marsh and his arch enemy Edward Cope (right) were bitter rivals in their attempts to outdo each other in discovering the most dinosaur fossils.

great scheme of Earth's history? Back in the 1700s, Buffon had imagined an ever-changing Earth that had existed long before humans appeared on the scene. He further imagined that long period as a time for the preparation of mankind. In other words, Adam and Eve were not brought onto the scene by God until the world had become "worthy of mankind's rule."

As early as 1800 stone tools, such as hand axes, were being dug up in England and Europe, and they were found side by side with the fossils of extinct animals. Some such stone tools were being unearthed soon after Darwin returned from his voyage aboard the *Beagle*. The tools, the fossils of extinct animals, and the fossil remains of humans were much older than interpretations of the Bible permitted them to be. With such discoveries, the science of paleontology was forced to admit fossil human beings among its ranks. One very big question had to be asked: As animal and plant species living today were shown to have fossil ancestors different from their modern forms, was it possible that human beings living today also had fossil ancestors different from their modern forms? What would the fossil record show?

Dubois Finds an "Ape-Man"

By the late 1880s Darwin's ideas about evolution had gained general acceptance by most scientists around the world. In 1871, just before Marsh and Cope declared war, Darwin published *The Descent of Man and Selection in Relation to Sex*. The book showed in great detail common patterns in body plan among apes, humans, and certain other species. Humans, Darwin said, also had evolved, right along with all the other members of the animal kingdom. He further said that apes and humans had evolved from a common ancestor.

A young Dutch military doctor named Eugène Dubois was

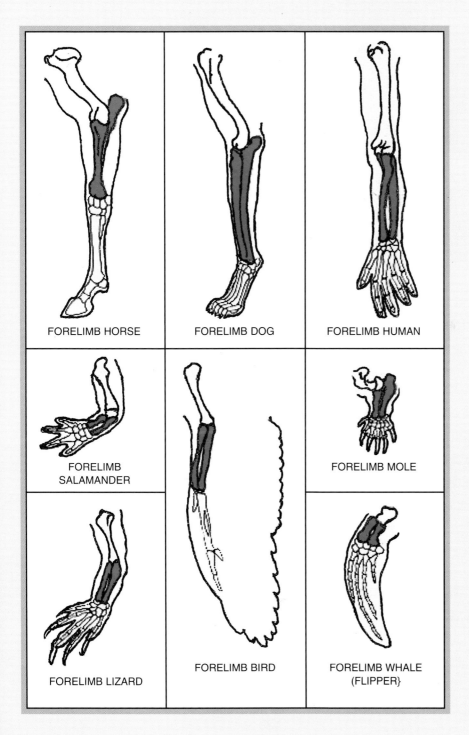

FORELIMB HORSE

FORELIMB DOG

FORELIMB HUMAN

FORELIMB SALAMANDER

FORELIMB MOLE

FORELIMB LIZARD

FORELIMB BIRD

FORELIMB WHALE (FLIPPER)

The limb bones of horses, dogs, humans, and the other species shown here clearly are very similar variations on a common limb bone pattern of a common ancestor millions of years old. There can be no other logical explanation. Similar observations over a wide variety of fossils and living species convinced scientists of the late 1800s, that Darwin's theory of evolution was essentially correct.

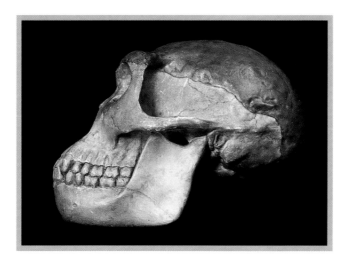

Java Man was the name given to the skull discovered by Eugene Dubois in 1891. Dubois was searching for a "missing link" between modern humans and apes, and he found one. Java Man turned out to be 700,000 years old and was later given the scientific name Homo erectus, meaning "upright man."

fascinated by Darwin's book. He vowed to find the "missing link" between apes and humans. By the late 1880s only about a half dozen fossils of humans were known. Dubois was sent to Java, north of Australia, and that's where he began to dig for his missing link. In 1891 his workers unearthed the lower part of a skull near the village of Trinil. Over the next two years, he found a molar tooth and part of an upper leg bone. He was convinced that his three fossils were from some early human type, not from an ape. Popularly known as Java Man, Dubois's fossils later were given the scientific name *Homo erectus* and were shown to be 700,000 years old. His remarkable discovery quickly gained world attention and flung the door into our human past wide open.

The Piltdown Hoax

By the early 1900s, human fossil finds had pushed our human ancestry well back into Earth's ancient history, and interest in missing links between humans and apes was high. Around 1908 an English amateur paleontologist named Charles Dawson found pieces of a human skull that had been dug out of a gravel pit in

Piltdown, Sussex. Over the next few years more bits of skull were found, along with part of an apelike lower jaw. And there were a few crude stone tools and some mammal fossils.

By 1912 a scientist at the British Museum of Natural History pieced together the apelike jaw and human skull pieces and named them Dawson's Dawn Man. In the years that followed there were many arguments over the Piltdown skull. One problem was that the pieces of the jawbone that were supposed to fit up against the lower skull had been broken off, so there was no way to be sure that the two pieces really came from the same animal. Finally, in 1953 the Piltdown skull was shown conclusively to be a fake, a hoax. The skull fragments were those of a modern human, the teeth of the jaw had been filed down, and the jaw-

"The man who never was" best describes the so-called Piltdown Man. A prankster cleverly buried an ape jawbone along with part of a human skull in an attempt to fool scientists in the early 1900s, and he did. The prankster was never identified.

bone was that of an ape, stained to look much older than it actually was. Someone had cleverly planted the skull fragments, jaw, mammal fossils, and crude tools in the gravel pit.

The hoaxer was never found, but many felt that Dawson must have been involved in some way. Why would someone want to go to all that trouble? An answer has yet to be found.

While the mystery of Piltdown Man was being debated, it was given much attention in newspapers. If the hoax ended on a positive note, it's that "for the first time it brought the human fossil record squarely into the public eye and established it as a major source of media interest," according to anthropologist Ian Tattersall, of The American Museum of Natural History.

The "Beat-up Chimpanzee" and Lucy

While they were trying to figure out who Piltdown Man was, a remarkable human fossil find in South Africa pushed the ancestral age of humans still further back in time and raised new questions about our human ancestry. In 1924 miners discovered a fossil skull encased in sand, rocks, and lime. The skull was taken to Professor Raymond Dart, head of the Anatomy Department at Witwatersrand University in South Africa. Dart soon realized that he was gazing on "one of the most significant finds ever made in the history of anthropology," he later wrote.

Most of Dart's professional colleagues in Europe disagreed. One anthropologist looked at the fossil and said it was "just a somewhat beat-up chimpanzee." The skull turned out to be that of a five- or six-year-old child between one and two million years old. It was named *Australopithecus*, or "southern ape." More ape-like than human, it was the earliest human ancestor then known.

Dart became famous overnight. By this time, the entire scientific community had become fascinated by each new discovery that not only pushed back the age of our human ancestry but also was beginning to provide tantalizing glimpses into human evolution.

In the summer of 1959, the highly respected paleoanthropologist Louis Leakey shocked his colleagues when he announced a new find that showed that early true humans lived some two million years ago. The fossil human bones that he found came from Olduvai Gorge, in southern Africa. Until that time, Dubois' Java Man, a mere 700,000 years old, was thought to be the earliest true human. Leakey's find was important for three reasons. First, it pushed the appearance of early humans back more than a million years. Second, it supported the theory that humans evolved in Africa, and not in Asia, as some believed. Third, it showed that early humans lived at the same time as Dart's *Australopithecus*.

Louis Leakey has gotten most of the credit for the Olduvai fossils. Many of the finds were in fact made by his wife, Mary Leakey. Since 1972, when Louis died, Mary, Louis and Mary's son Richard, and Richard's wife Meave, have continued to dig up and study fossils of early humans and their ancestors in East Africa. Mary has also traced the development of the earliest and most primitive stone tools, which were used for chopping and cutting, to more sophisticated axes and knives.

In 1924 Raymond Dart became the first person to recognize that a skull found in a lime quarry in South Africa represented an early stage of human evolution. The new humanlike species was named Australopithecus africanus, *meaning "southern ape of Africa." The remains are some three million years old.*

The discoveries of Dart and the Leakeys shook paleoanthropology to its roots, but a find made in 1974 caused an even greater stir. In November of that year, anthropologist Donald C. Johanson, of the Institute of Human Origins in Berkeley, California, unearthed a remarkable fossil skeleton. The find pushed the date of the then earliest known *hominids* back to 3.2 million years. Hominids are apelike and humanlike creatures that walk upright on two legs.

The discovery took place in Hadar, Ethiopia. The skeleton was that of a female who stood 3 feet 8 inches (112 centimeters) tall and weighed about 65 pounds (29 kilograms). She had a mixture of ape and human features. "Her long arms dangled apelike by her side," Johanson later wrote in *National Geographic* magazine. He named her Lucy, after the Beatles song, "Lucy in the Sky with Diamonds." Lucy was given the scientific name *Australopithecus afarensis*, meaning "southern ape of Afar." Lucy was more apelike than humanlike, but her importance as a fossil in our human ancestral line is that she and her companions are now thought to have given rise to all other hominids after her, including us.

For a while it looked as though Lucy was the oldest hominid, but she was to be toppled from her place in the sky. In 1994 volcanic ash layers near Kenya's Lake Turkana revealed three large fossil teeth, then a nearly complete set of teeth from the creature's lower jaw. That was enough for anthropologists to know that the apelike owner was an even older hominid. They named it *Australopithecus anamensis*. Meave Leakey found more *anamensis* fossils in an area of East Africa called Kanapoi that same year. To date, a total of fifty-nine *anamensis* fossil bones have been found. They suggest a mix between chimplike and humanlike features. The fossils turned out to be 4.1 million years old.

In 1974 Donald C. Johanson uncovered the bones of a female hominid in Ethiopia. He named them Lucy, who turned out to be 3.2 million years old. When alive, Lucy weighed about 65 pounds (30 kilograms). She was given the scientific name of Australopithecus afaransis and had a mixture of ape and human features, as shown in an artist's version of what her kind might have looked like when she lived.

Also in 1994, Tim White, of the University of California at Berkeley, found an even older hominid while digging at the Aramis site in Ethiopia. White's fossil was dated at 4.4 million years old.

Right now no one can say how many still older species will be found to fill the gap between true apes and the first true hominids, but each year new fossil finds are helping us to find out. Steno, Cuvier, Darwin, and all the others would be fascinated to learn how those mere "fish seeds" of the old Greeks are helping scientists unravel one of the most fascinating science mysteries—that of our human origins.

The oldest creature in the line of humans descendants is now thought to be one called "Dawn Ape," or Aegyptopithecus zeuxis. *Its fossil skull remains were found in the Egyptian desert and are about 3.3 million years old.*

Seven

How Fossils Are Formed and Dated

Fossils come in many different forms. *Body fossils* are the remains of animals or plants that used to be alive. Examples include bones, petrified wood, and amber. *Trace fossils* are evidence left by a once-living animal or plant rather than actual parts of the plant or animal. Dinosaur footprints, fossilized worm burrows, and shell imprints in rock are trace fossils.

From Bones to Minerals

Although fossils may seem common, they actually are rare, if you consider the huge number of ancient critters that ever lived but never became fossils. When most living things die, they decompose and vanish without a trace. Usually it is only the hard parts, such as bone, hard wood, or shells that become fossils, so you wouldn't expect to find many fossils of things like jellyfish. But even hard materials become fossils only under just the right conditions.

If too much time passes before the materials are completely covered, even hard materials such as bone decompose.

Imagine a *Stegosaurus* that died 150 million years ago in present-day West Virginia. Just before it dies, it walks through a shallow mud flat and leaves footprints. Within a few hours, scavenger dinosaurs come along and eat their dead friend. In the process, they snap its bones and scatter them about, but they don't disturb the footprints. The warm air dries them out. Blowing sand, dust, and other sediments fill in and cover the footprints.

Many millions of years pass. More and more sediments keep piling up over the broken bones and footprints. During rainy periods and floods, minerals dissolved in the water seep down through the sediments. When the water evaporates, the minerals remain and act as a cement that helps turn the sediments to stone. Pressure from the now thick layers of sediments above also helps turn the lower sediments to stone.

During those millions of years something else has been happening. Molecule by molecule, minerals seeping through the sediments have replaced the bone fragments as water has dissolved the original bone. The footprints also have been preserved over that long time period. The mud flat, too, has been compressed and turned to sedimentary rock. Fossil hunters 150 million years later stumble onto the scene and find the newly exposed scattered fossils of *Stegosaurus*. They also find casts of the animal's footprints.

Those fossils are the remains of the geological time period called the Jurassic. Since the time of Cuvier, geologists have deciphered Earth's geologic history based on the sequence of fossils as they are found at various depths in the ground. Knowing the age of the fossils and the rocks that contain them, we have been able to make a geologic calendar that shows scenes from the

HOW
FOSSILS
ARE
FORMED
AND
DATED

Glistening a silvery gold, this remarkable fossil of an animal known as an ammonite is a spectacular example of mineral replacement in fossil formation. As the shell of the original animal (tan inset) decayed, it was slowly replaced by minerals, in this case iron pyrite, which is also known as "fool's gold." Ammonites were very common during the Triassic Period, so common that their fossil remains have been used to map the borders of Mesozoic seas.

great pageant of life that has unfolded from the time our planet was formed some 4.6 billion years ago. Most of the story has come to light only over the past two hundred years, since the time Cuvier, Smith, Darwin, and the many others first began to fit the endless pieces of the geologic puzzle together.

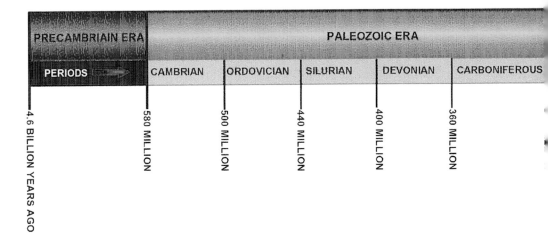

The geologic ages of Earth span time from Earth's formation as a planet
some 4.6 billion years ago through to the present. Eras, which are read

Telling the Age of Fossils

How can geologists tell whether this or that fossil is 700,000 years
old, or whether it is 200 million years old from the Mesozoic Era
and the Triassic Period? No one, of course, knows *exactly* how
old any fossil is. All we can do is make an estimate, but our esti-
mates keep getting better as new or improved dating techniques
come along.

It wasn't until the early 1900s that we learned to estimate
how many years old a plant or animal fossil was. That age in years
is called *absolute age*. Your absolute age may be ten or twelve or
thirty years. But there is another kind of age called *relative age*. If
you have a younger sister, then your relative age is greater than
hers. Recall that William Smith around 1800 became skilled at
telling the relative ages of the fossils he discovered at various
depths in the ground. The fossils near the surface were relatively
younger than fossils buried deeper down. In that way paleontologists knew that fishes as a group were relatively older than reptiles,

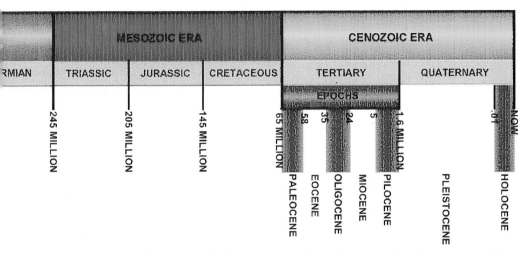

	MESOZOIC ERA			CENOZOIC ERA	
RMIAN	TRIASSIC	JURASSIC	CRETACEOUS	TERTIARY	QUATERNARY

EPOCHS

245 MILLION | 205 MILLION | 145 MILLION | 65 MILLION | 58 | 35 | 24 | 5 | 1.6 MILLION | .01 | NOW

PALEOCENE
EOCENE
OLIGOCENE
MIOCENE
PLIOCENE
PLEISTOCENE
HOLOCENE

across the top, are broken down into Periods such as the Cambrian and the Devonian. After the Cretaceous, Periods are further broken down into Epochs.

and that reptiles were relatively older than mammals, and so on. But during Smith's time no one knew the absolute age of any of those fossils. Because people of the 1600s and 1700s, for instance, had no way of knowing the absolute age of Earth rocks, no matter where they were found, they turned to the only geologic "calendar" they had, the Bible.

To estimate the absolute age of a fossil or the rock containing the fossil, we need special tools and special knowledge about how atoms behave. By the early 1900s scientists were experimenting with radioactive elements, which are made up of large and unstable atoms. The atoms are said to be "unstable" because they decay by shooting off some of their tiny particles called neutrons and protons. When that happens, the atoms of one radioactive element turn into atoms of a different radioactive element. For instance, the radioactive element uranium-238 decays into the radioactive element thorium-234 by shooting off two neutrons and two protons. We call the original element the parent element and the new element the daughter element.

We know of several radioactive parent elements that decay into daughter elements. Potassium-40 turns into argon-40. Carbon-14 turns into nitrogen-14. We also know how long it takes the changes to occur. If you have a chunk of pure potassium-40, you would have to wait 1.3 billion years for half of its atoms to turn into argon-40 atoms. We say that potassium-40 has a *half-life* of 1.3 billion years.

This radioactive element	changes into this	and has a half-life of
uranium-238	lead-206	4,510 million years
potassium-40	argon-40	1,300 million years
rubidium-87	strontium-87	50,000 years
carbon-14	nitrogen-14	5,730 years

Any rock you pick up has some atoms of radioactive parent elements. It also has some daughter-element atoms. By comparing the number of parent atoms with daughter atoms we can say how long the parent element has been losing protons. That means we can say how old the rock is, or its absolute age. Over the years since 1900, chemists have developed several different methods of dating rocks. Some methods work for rocks that are many millions of years old. Other methods work only for relatively younger rocks. The carbon-14 method of dating, for instance, is good only for fossils less than 30,000 years old. So if we use the carbon-14 dating method and learn that a fossil is 25,000 years old, then we also know that the rock that contains the fossil must also be 25,000 years old.

But how can we learn the age of a fossil that has lost all of its carbon? If we use the potassium-argon method and learn that

HOW
FOSSILS
ARE
FORMED
AND
DATED

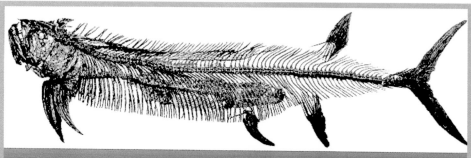

Last meal. In late Cretaceous seas of some 70 million years ago that covered Kansas, a 15-foot-long fish named Portheous *gulped down a smaller fish named* Gillicus. *Right after the meal,* Portheous *died, was covered over, and became a famous fossil. The smaller fish can clearly be seen in* Portheous's *stomach in the fossil skeleton imprints at top and bottom.*

67

Suppose you are an archaeologist and dig up the remains of a campsite that you suspect is several thousand years old. Your problem is to measure its age by using the carbon-14 dating technique.

How Old Is That Piece of Wood?

First you select a piece of old wood about the weight of a jackknife from the campsite. Next you cut a piece exactly the same weight from a living tree. You have an instrument called a radiation counter and hold it next to the new piece of wood. The instrument begins to give off beeps, each beep signaling one carbon-14 atom changing into a nitrogen-14 atom. You carefully time the beeps for exactly one minute and count twenty beeps. Next you do the same thing with the old piece of wood, and it registers only ten beeps a minute. This would tell you that the old piece of wood had lost half the number of carbon-14 atoms it had when it was part of a living tree. Since it takes 5,730 years for half the carbon-14 atoms in a dead animal or plant to change into nitrogen-14, this tells you that the old wood was cut from a tree about 5,700 years ago.

HOW

FOSSILS

ARE

FORMED

AND

DATED

the rock that contains the fossil is 700,000 years old, then we know that the fossil must also be 700,000 years old, since the fossil had to be formed right along with its rock.

Before we had discovered radioactivity and applied our knowledge of it to the study of fossils, meteorites from Mars, Moon rocks, and Earth rocks, we could only make educated guesses about how old those pieces of the solar system were. Now we can assign an absolute age to just about anything we find on Earth or elsewhere. Just imagine how different the lives of Buffon, Cuvier, Darwin, and others would have been if they had been able to use radiometric age dating as they formed their hypotheses. As we keep improving ways of measuring the ages of fossils, we become better able to fit together more and more pieces in the puzzle of Earth's history.

URANIUM - 238 — 92 PROTONS 146 NEUTRONS — 2 PROTONS — 2 NEUTRONS — THORIUM - 234 — 90 PROTONS 144 NEUTRONS

Radioactive elements making up certain rocks can be used to tell the rocks' age. Each radioactive element has its own rate of decay into a different element. For example, the radioactive element uranium-238 decays into the radioactive element thorium-234. This happens whenever an atom of uranium casts off two protons and two neutrons. It is characteristic of extremely large atoms, such as uranium, to be unstable and so turn into less complex and, therefore, more stable elements.

Eight

The New Catastrophism

Scientists have identified five major periods in Earth's history during which untold millions of plant and animal species became extinct. It now seems that each of these periods of mass dying was brought on by sharp, planetwide environmental changes. Some scientists believe we are going through another such period today.

The most recent previous period of extinction was about 65 million years ago and was marked by a giant asteroid striking the planet in what is now the Gulf of Mexico off the coast of Yucatán. It left a crater some 110-180 miles (180-300 kilometers) across, called the Chicxulub crater. The impact rattled Earth, hurling untold tons of rock, dust, powdered clay, and other materials high into the air. The dust was then caught up in the global air currents and carried far and wide. During the months before it settled to the ground, it blocked out sunlight and changed Earth's climate. It now seems that the lives of the dinosaurs, along with those of numerous other animal groups, were snuffed out by the cosmic catastrophe. Some paleontologists, however, believe that the dinosaurs had already been on their way out and that the asteroid impact simply finished them off.

A worldwide layer of clay rich in the element iridium is evidence for such a shattering impact. Earth's rocks contain relatively little iridium, but certain metallic asteroids and comets are rich sources of the element. When scientists discovered an especially rich layer of iridium in the clays marking the 65-million-year level in Earth's rock strata, it seemed highly likely that the rare element was dust from an asteroid impact.

Catastrophism Today

Fossil evidence supports a blend of Cuvier's catastrophism and Hutton's uniformitarianism. It goes by the names neocatastrophism, punctuated evolution, and punctuated equilibrium. Although Earth's history may be marked mostly by Hutton-style uniformitarianism—slow and steady change—every now and then asteroid or comet impacts produce sudden and drastic environmental change. Many such changes in the past have created environmental opportunities that have favored relatively rapid evolutionary changes in plants and animals. Hence the expression "punctuated equilibrium," which suggests occasional, brief spurts of evolutionary change, rather than the uninterrupted slow pace of change imagined by Darwin.

What can we expect to learn from fossils in the future? Only the future can tell. It is tempting to think that most of the big questions have already been answered. We have what seems to be a very reliable estimate of Earth's age: 4.6 billion years. And the layering of fossils in Earth's rock strata has revealed at least a broad outline of what living things have come and gone over that vast time span and how they have changed.

And why are fossils so important? Like a 3-D puzzle with no instructions, fossils tell the tale of how, over the past 3.5 billion years, life on Earth developed from tiny bacterial cells to include all of the plants and animals we see around us today. To the people who study them, fossils are reminders of just how long our planet Earth has been supporting life. On this time scale, the ten thousand years since the last ice age is no more than a small blip. It might seem that all that remains is to fill in gaps and details so that we have a smooth and detailed reading of our planet's history rather than only a broad and spotty outline.

A number of scientists of the 1700s were smug in their knowledge, thinking that they had learned just about all there was to be learned about the universe and that what they didn't know was unknowable. One French scientist, for instance, said, "Never will we ever be able to learn the chemical composition of the stars." How wrong he was. To date, we have barely scratched Earth's surface to reveal its fossil treasures. Every year exciting new fossil finds add to our human history as a species. And each find not only helps answer old questions, but it opens up a host of new questions. Science is a never-ending search, with no promise that all the answers will ever be found. Two hundred years from now people may look back at the state of science at the beginning of the twenty-first century and marvel at how little we understood. The new questions science poses with each new discovery are what at once makes science so rewarding and so wonderfully frustrating.

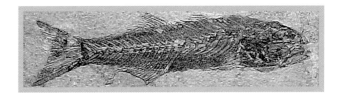

Absolute age—the age of a thing, measured in years. Absolute ages of fossils are measured using sophisticated equipment and are stated in thousands or millions of years.

Adaptation—a trait within a plant or animal population that makes it more suited for its environment; the Act or process of adapting, especially to environmental circumstances.

Anatomist—someone who studies the shape and structure of living things; such study is called the science of anatomy.

Body fossil—remains of part of a plant or animal that lived more than 10,000 years ago.

Cast—any substance that has hardened after filling in a mold. The cast has the same shape as the original object.

Cold-blooded—lacking metabolic, or internal, means of regulating body temperature; typical of modern reptiles and amphibians.

Catastrophism—the theory that natural catastrophes, such as floods, earthquakes, and volcanic eruptions, have changed the face of Earth throughout our planet=s history.

Culture—A common language, history, and set of beliefs shared by members of a population.

Eternalism—The idea that time has no beginning and no end.

Evolution—The various patterns of biological change that ultimately cause the success (adaptation) or failure (extinction) of species and produce new species of plants and animals.

Extinction—The dying of all of the members of a species of plant or animal. Once a species has become extinct, it is gone forever.

Daughter elements—elements that result from the decay of radioactive elements. By measuring the ratio of parent atoms to daughter atoms in a sample fossil, scientists can determine its absolute age.

Fossils—from Latin *fossilis*, meaning "something dug out of the ground." Fossils are the remains of once-living plants or animals. They may be bits of bone or teeth or even footprints or other imprints. Almost all fossils are found in sedimentary rock and are considered more than 10,000 years old.

Geology—from the Greek *geo*, meaning "Earth", and *logos*, meaning "study." The science of the study of Earth, what it is made of, and how its materials change over time.

Halflife—the time it takes for one-half of the atoms of a radioactive element to change into a different element.

Hominid—any member of the human family that walks upright on two legs. Modern humans are the only surviving hominids.

Hypothesis—an idea that needs to be tested to find out whether it is valid or not.

Mineral—any element or compound found naturally in Earth, formed by a nonliving process, having a fairly uniform chemical makeup, a rather constant set of physical properties, and a fixed and orderly internal arrangement of its atoms.

Mold—a hollow impression of the shape of an object that once filled the space.

Organic—any material that is or was once part of living matter.

Paleoanthropologist—an anthropologist who studies the physical features and cultures of ancient peoples in an attempt to trace the evolution of human beings.

Paleontologist—a scientist who specializes in the recovery and study of fossils.

Paleontology—the science concerned with the study of fossils of life forms that have existed throughout geologic time.

Parent elements—atoms of unstable radioactive elements that decay into different (daughter) elements by emitting protons and neutrons.

Relative age—the placement of an object on a time line described as eras, periods, and epochs before or after younger or older objects.

Sedimentary rock—rock formed from clay, lime, sand, gravel, or plant or animal remains that have been squeezed together under great pressure or naturally cemented for long periods of time.

Sediments—loose materials such as clay, mud, sand, gravel, lime, and other Earth materials eroded from rocks and moved elsewhere by wind, water, and ice and left behind.

Stratum (*pl.* strata)—layer of rock.

Theory—a hypothesis that has been reliably supported by many observations.

Trace fossil—Indirect evidence, but not parts, of plants or animals that lived at least 10,000 years ago. These include footprints, feces, burrows, and tubes dug by worms, shrimp, and crabs, for example.

Uniformitarianism—the theory that Earth's surface has been changed and continues to be changed by the same kinds of processes, such as erosion, volcanism, earthquake activity, and rising and falling seas, for example, that have been changing Earth since it was first formed.

Warm-blooded—possessing the metabolic means of regulating body temperature.

Further Reading

Asimov, Isaac. *Asimov's Chronology of Science & Discovery*. New York: Harper Collins. 1989.

Bower, Bruce. "High-tech Images Shrink Fossil Braincase." *Science News* (June 13, 1998) p. 374.

Colbert, Edwin H. *Men and Dinosaurs*, New York: E. P. Dutton & Co., Inc., 1968.

Gallant, Roy A. *Charles Darwin: The Making of a Scientist*. Garden City, NY: Doubleday & Company, Inc. 1972

———. *The Day the Sky Split Apart*. New York: Macmillan, 1995.

———. *Early Humans*. Tarrytown, NY: Marshall Cavendish, 2000.

———. *Fossils*. New York: Franklin Watts, 1985.

———. *How Life Began: Creation vs. Evolution*. New York: Four Winds Press, 1975.

Galant, Roy A. and Christopher J. Schuberth. *Discovering Rocks and Minerals*. New York: Natural History Press, 1967.

Gore, Rick. "Expanding Worlds." The Dawn of Humans Series. *National Geographic*. (May 1997) pp. 84–109.

———. "The First Europeans." The Dawn of Humans Series. *National Geographic* (July 1997) pp. 96–113.

———. "The First Steps." The Dawn of Humans Series. *National Geographic* (February 1997) pp. 72–99.

———. "Extinctions." *National Geographic* (June 1989) pp. 662–698.

Hoffmann, Hillel J. "Messel: Window on an Ancient World." *National Geographic*. (February 2000) pp. 34–51.

Jaffee, Mark. *The Gilded Dinosaur: The Fossil War Between E. D. Cope and O. C. Marsh and the Rise of American Science*. New York: Crown, 2000.

Leakey, Meave. "The Farthest Horizon," The Dawn of Humans. *National Geographic* (September 1995) pp. 38–51.

Lewin, Roger. *Bones of Contention: Controversies in the Search for Human Origins*. Chicago: University of Chicago Press, 1987.

Ley, Willy. *Dragons in Amber*. New York: Viking Press, 1951.

———. *Dawn of Zoology*. Englewood Cliffs, N.J.: Prentice-Hall, Inc., 1968.

Monastersky, Richard. "Chunk of Death-Dealing Asteroid Found." *Science News* (November 21, 1998) p. 324.

Rudwick, Martin J. *The Meaning of Fossils*. 2nd ed. New York: Science History Publications, a division of Neale Watson Academic Publications, Inc. 1976

Russell, Bertrand. *Religion and Science*. London: Oxford University Press, 1935.

Tattersall, Ian. *The Fossil Trail*. New York: Oxford University Press, 1995.

Wallace, David Rains. *The Bonehunters' Revenge: Dinosaurs, Greed, and the Greatest Scientific Feud of the Gilded Age*. HM, 1999.

Try these websites for information about fossils and about the many fossil-related topics included in this book.

www.ucmp.berkeley.edu University of California at Berkeley.

www.amnh.org American Museum of Natural History.

www.talkorigins.org A usernet newsgroup devoted to discussions of evolution and the creationists points of view.

www.cyberspacemuseum.com Yale Peabody Musuem.

Index

Page numbers for illustrations are in **boldface**.